A Treatment

Ann Shenfield

Ann Shenfield works across a range of media. Her poems have received various awards, including the Judith Wright Poetry Prize for her book *You Can Get Only So Close On Google Earth*, which was also a finalist for the Queensland Premier's Literary Awards. Her poetry has been longlisted for the Peter Porter Prize and the ACU Poetry Prize.

Ann's animated films have also received various prizes and have screened at numerous festivals, including selection to the Official Competition at the Berlin International Film Festival.

This book was written on the traditional land of the Wurundjeri people of the Kulin nation. I acknowledge the Traditional Owners and pay respect to Elders past, present and emerging. I recognise that sovereignty was never ceded on the sacred land that I live, work on and love, and believe this needs to be addressed and redressed.

Ann Shenfield

A Treatment

UPSWELL

First published in Australia in 2023
by Upswell Publishing
Perth, Western Australia
upswellpublishing.com

ISBN: 978-0-645-53696-6

A catalogue record for this
book is available from the
National Library of Australia

Cover design by Chil3, Fremantle
Typeset in Foundry Origin by Lasertype

Upswell Publishing is assisted by the State of Western Australia
through its funding program for arts and culture.

Department of
**Local Government, Sport
and Cultural Industries**
GOVERNMENT OF
WESTERN AUSTRALIA

Contents

1.   9

A treatment   11

Sophia does not hold up the world   13

On seeing a woman who resembles me in
a photo of the liberation of Ravensbrück   15

Playing scrabble with my mother   17

From a remove   18

The man who healed hearts   20

The new world   21

Synonyms   23

Implementing a final solution requires breakfast   25

Sometimes, a dog   26

Versions of a snowflake   28

Quantifiable data   31

End to end   33

From some other place   36

2.   39

She says   41

It was always the voice of I want   42

Who   43

It's easier   44

The fig tree   45

Someone who isn't   46

Resistance   47

The first morning   48

Phantoms   52

The phone rings   54

Form   55

On arctic foxes and snow owls   56

Magnifications   57

Documenting clouds   58

A photo of a photo   60

Signs of weakness   62

In the air   63

It was the lightest of touch   64

Rock   66

In the time   68

Dinosaurs   69

Outside   70

For what seems like weeks   71

In red blankets   72

It's spring   73

Sway   74

3.   77

Somewhere then   79

My relationship to profanity may be
different to yours   82

Someone threw a rock   84

And did I tell you   85

Like swallows   87

The language of birds   89

Curfew   91

Dandelions   93

Those people in metros in places with
names you can't properly pronounce   95

The ways of crows   98

The way I need to write now   101

Seven facts   103

Goodnight moon   104

In the twilight   105

Sunflowers   106

Acknowledgements   107

1.

A treatment

In 1938 in fascist Italy the man credited
with initiating electroconvulsive therapy

—Ugo Cerletti—observes pigs in an abattoir
being stunned before their slaughter

My mother is in pre-war Poland
the family haven't yet fled to Russia

She still has all the hopes
and dreams of a nine-year-old

Meanwhile Ugo discerns that stunned
pigs appear less agitated

He surmises they accept their demise
more amenably when shocked

And he thinks, *why not?*
besides he's already tried a version on dogs

Placing cables in their mouths and anuses
but this only leads to cardiac arrest

This is how some of it evolved
and me, a dog lover and vegetarian

Trying to piece together a mother
grieving her husband's sudden heart failure

Later they will notice that shock
treatment messes with a person's affect

How it no longer matches the emotions
think vacancy for tears, laughter for anguish

Though I worry, might this
also be true for pigs?

They diagnosed my mother's guilt
and grief as depression

Then stunned her to a silence
the Italian died a year before her shocks

The Sorbonne gave him an honorary degree
my mother came home but didn't properly return

Sophia does not hold up the world

                                        like Atlas
she is only an appendage, a suffix to philo—

Incomplete in her own terms, almost wisdom
but without mythic status

Still, I know that wisdom walks
with frostbitten toes across tundras

To places with names that no longer exist
where at a border crossing she prevents a shooting

Let's say this act saves the entire group
in that snowed-in Slavic nowhere

Only discoverable now in outdated maps
a story, part fairytale, or almost oral history

Except she never spoke of it, or of how
as an ex-school mistress she would accept

Whatever work was delegated
like at the factory peeling potatoes

While wisdom grieved a husband
before she would learn of the others

The twenty-four who tapered
into two—this mother and her child

Sophia does not hold up the world
though she sends food parcels

To her one surviving nephew in a gulag
—parcels that enable him to endure

If you save a life, you save the whole world
my people are fond of saying

Though I hesitate to mention Sophia's plan
it was only that her child who'd become my mother

Was afraid of water, that they didn't wave
or, that is, drown

Besides, in those circumstances
who wouldn't consider suicidal ideation wise?

This world is always being held up by Atlas
even if Sophia, in Polish it's Zofia, realises me

*written in response to Damon O'Brien's *Atlas Carried the World*

On seeing a woman who resembles me in a photo of the liberation of Ravensbrück

there's a woman who looks like me, in black and white
with my eyes, my chin, and the way I look when it's cold

in November 1941, in Ravensbrück
Dr Friedrich Mennecke referred to the women

he chose to live or die, as representative portions
like shapes, that he called *forms*—

and here now I see my *form* in her
she stares away from me through barbed wire

and although I don't know her, I see myself
imprisoned in the lake district in Germany

I know language enables distance
and normalises the aberrant

words can shift the sentient into stock
still I don't know how to assimilate

seeing me in her, or is it her in me?
ravens are considered harbingers

though the truth is they're known
to think like humans

once I saw a raven clutch
a lorikeet beside the Merri Creek

I can't distinguish one raven from another
yet I know they recognise my *form*

Playing scrabble with my mother

She makes sense of words
through the filter of sounds
that are not the same to me

So the words are not
as I usually understand them
I say, *Which i do you mean?*

*Is it **i** with a dot or **ai** for apple?*
It all sounds the same to her
like versions of blue in Russia

Or my *yanny* to your *laurel*
or how in Hungary, my friend said
they describe the sky as azure-green

The afternoon turns Prussian blue
and she says, *I have strange dreams*
where I am my father's daughter

I say, *But that's you—you know*
and she says, *But you're there too*
then she clarifies

It's like, I am the daughter and you
are the mother, in words I hear
but can no longer parse

From a remove

The woman with the styrofoam cup and no teeth
sits all day at the taxi rank and is *a local identity*

The driver tells me in his practised monologue
he tells me she lost everything in the war

was forced to grow vegetables for soldiers
slave labour, you know—

How she had nothing
but when the Russians came

she lost everything all over again
How do you lose nothing?

I think about asking, but he's still
talking about her sitting there

with her no teeth, her free cup of coffee,
and her swearing, so I can't help but float

to my mother, her new teeth
and my grandmother's face

how I recognise it now
in the shape of my mother

except she must have been
there all along, staring

at me from a remove
like the vacant blue sky

with its constance of stars or that
woman with her everything

and her nothing
all over again.

The man who healed hearts

A few days before I receive the letter I read
about Alexis Carrel, the Nobel Prize winner

He'd visited Lourdes and believed in miracles
later, he emigrated from France to America

Wikipedia says he used *experimental* animals
to develop vascular, then open-heart surgery

I don't read of him in this context though
—it's his book on eugenics *Man, The Unknown*

Which advocated the use of gas
on criminals and the criminally insane

A text that proved influential
its reach would extend to—

Samuel, Lutka, Genia, Mania, Tamara, Cywia
these names—like closed books to me

In her twenties a doctor told my grandmother
her constitution would never be strong

Yet she lived to ninety-seven and recited
those murdered siblings' details every night

The letter about my heart says, *Her high genetic
risk cannot ever be completely mitigated*

My grandmother's trauma was not mine
but something of the unknown insists

The new world

A friend says she thinks of you
as if you're in America

And reminds me of the dream you had
—you were behind the airport gates

Months later another mutual friend visits
Tanzania where a Maasai guide takes her

To a place near Kilimanjaro
where Polish Jews escaped in 1942

The friend says that in an uprising
the Jews were mistaken

For German hegemonists
and were massacred

She says you would have
appreciated the irony

And that you'd always
wanted to visit Zanzibar

The friend sends me photos
of elephants, giraffes, zebras

And a lion who is dozing
among purple flowers

I've read that the Maasai
are becoming less nomadic

And that elephants are moving
inexorably to extinction

It's unbridgeable this distance
now you're in America

Synonyms

To attempt to see beyond the generic
past trees, plants, birds, as synonyms for *nature*

psychologists say that in the former Soviet Republic
people overlook the nuance in consumables

raspberry, lemon, orange and cola
are all equated as one thing—*soda*

and when I bring my mother an array of cakes
vanilla slice, eclair, peach danish, fruit tart

she considers them all, then invariably says
I don't mind, you choose

the assortment peters into one thing—*cake*
so I choose for her

she sends me emails of her life story
and labels them—*the saga*

I reinterpret her lived history
switch focus to the lyrical

a child's perception of war
as improbable as any fairytale

re-vision it through my limited prism
though over time the scenery shifts to life

the bird calls weave a tapestry of sound
each mynah an individual—each its own song

this day then might stand for any other
but on Friday night I give my mother

half an apple strudel, and some cheesecake
then try to sit within the moment

to listen, or endeavour to not seek more
starvation calls from deep within a mother

Implementing a final solution requires breakfast

The villa at Wannsee is palatial
yet unremarkable

The view overlooks immaculate gardens
towards the bay

An archived memo from the conference says
A light breakfast will be served

The gardens at Wannsee are neat and rectangular
these thoughts—chaotic and circular

Sometimes, a dog

This is how it is sometimes, a dog
a dog, this is how it is sometimes

each morning a dog and then sometimes
how it is, is the way it is now

when there's a dog who's in-between
being-and-not-being a dog

and sometimes this is how it is
how you have to repeat things

or that is, words and phrases
like I'm just going to take one step

at a time and for a moment the dog
is still a dog that stumbles and rights herself

and in that second or sometime then
there's a phone call, it's your mother

except, she sounds like she's someone else
or that is, someone else's mother

the dog is slipping and you're thinking
it's cruel to do this to any animal

that this is an example of Descartes's evil demon god
as you stand there listening to this simulacrum mother

telling you her urgent story and all the while
you're thinking that sometimes, sometimes it's like this

everything slippery, like the floorboards
the dog keeps stumbling over and your mother

if she is still your mother, telling you this story
that's long and convoluted and while she's speaking

you sense the house, as if in a landslide
everything slipping into everything else

while you, you just stand there
a breath, caught in the in-between

Versions of a snowflake

The snow
comes first
or is it
the unbroken
white
of a snow
covered
field?

Then it
occurs to you
that you don't know
the first thing
about snow
not how
it falls
or anything
like last year
when you were in
the falling
snow

You
realised
you'd misremembered
not just the way snow fell
but the shape
of snowflakes you had them
all wrong as well
You'd invented
your own version
of a snowflake
in much
the same way
you might imagine
someone else's
life

Like that girl
in the field
of unbroken white
who is a long
way off
too far
to ever be
your mother

Quantifiable data

Walking in the dog park
I have another conversation
with a man I call a western rationalist
but who prefers to be known as a scientist

When he starts saying *All things are knowable*
I'm not sure why our discussion
devolves into an argument
He says, *Everything is observable*

And quantifiable into data
while I say, *The way I see it*
we're more like ants, we can't ever
know everything, or that is, anything

We can't even imagine
colours that other creatures envisage
To which he says, *We can't see them*
but we can comprehend how and why

Then he starts to use words
like chromosome and phenotype
and I see myself drift towards
an unbridgeable invisibility

And later he says
You're **quite** *smart*
a qualifier I recognise
as diminishing

And I think about the ophthalmologist
who kept saying *good girl*
whenever I looked up or down
until I had no choice but to confront him

And even though he acknowledged
it was wrong, *It's just my background*
afterwards he began talking about aging and death
as if there was nothing between a girl and dying

I was trying to say to the western rationalist
I like things to be mysterious or the way an idea
can make its way unpredictably
into the world, like poetry

But it was as if we were shooting
through the sky like those stars
I saw in yesterday's meteor shower
which seemed to come out of nowhere

But were actually the tail of Halley's comet
as if knowing this makes it any more comprehensible
and why was it that when I watched those stars
I thought about my father and also about my mother?

In another observable moment of reality
where language might run in parallel
as I switch from a girl to dying
among other variables uncounted

End to end

It's no longer autumn
car headlights are streaming

Through the trees where
leaves used to be

Jo's father is preparing the garden
before he sells the house

My heart isn't really in it, he says
I know the first thing they'll do

Will be to take out the trees
then flatten the garden

Other houses in the street
already demolished

They build from end to end
and I can't face

The old magnolia or pruning
the overgrown passionfruit vine

- - - - - - - - -

My neighbour's grey kitten
is making her rounds

She resembles my first cat
perhaps they're related?

There's no way to know
but everywhere I look

There's a physical rewriting
and I wonder if people here

Aren't interested in retaining
what is someone else's story

or if every purchase
is a statement of transient intent?

The salvias bring in the birds, he says
and our garden boasts life

- - - - - - - -

The houses of my childhood
are also razed

Gooseberries, cherry plums
jacaranda trees

Flicker back and forward
with no one to corroborate the detail

Perhaps they never existed
or are all in my head

With only the birds who come and go
like the trees and the salvias

- - - - - - - - -

The car lights are clipped by the acacias
which have their own foreshadowing

There were people here before me
who have thought these thoughts

From some other place

I traded tamarillos
for a friend's Vietnamese mint

I'm not sure why but the word
tamarillo pleases me

like the sourness of its fruit
this year that tree was again supposed to die

but instead it held an abundant crop
of shiny red fruit which all hung festively

the lemon tree at my mother's house
has likewise never been more bountiful

and despite the winter frost, my favourite flower
a tiny purple sweet pea, has continued undaunted

there are moments then, where I prefer to think
it might all be connected

to my mother or with her unforeseen
December dying

while at times I fancy such things as signs
perhaps from her—who knows—

at others, they're just more evidence
of the overheating, more fodder for the usual despair

and while I hold both thoughts concurrently
yesterday I said about these patterns that emerge

in words—it's as if they're from some other place
as if it is my heart that's speaking

2.

She says

Lacan saw life as a poem
and although no one seems to fully
understand his writing

this one phrase resonates
as something you've always known
and you could say that poetry is life

but that isn't it
you recognise this as you walk
in the green-grey to the park

where the trees curve towards you
then fall away again and the frogmouths
that appear when no one's looking

that have been there all along
staring as they do at the black
with a gaze that sees the impenetrable

like words that spring from nowhere
or from the wind
or whatever's in the air

beneath everything
where nothing separates anyone
even in days when all the world

is isolated
this one true thing
walks you back towards life

It was always the voice of I want

and never the voice of wait and see
like the call of lorikeets
or the sound of wind in leaves

which the Japanese have a word for
like the sound that's underneath sound
or the voice that's beneath this voice

or the way she said, *you're still grieving*
and how I keep questioning those words
or like last night when everything

seemed to tingle on my periphery
and how just now it returned
a lake within a lake or as if

something were beneath this finitude
as I sit in my almost kitchen where the acacias
nod towards me and a lorikeet just called

Who

The tawnies are frog-mouthed birds
that people often mistake for owls

And since you need to spell it out
birds are beings in their own right—

Not solipsisms who can read your mind
because isn't that how you consider them?

Those night birds who appeared
in the park as if in response to your thoughts

As if you'd imagined them into being
then later when she says

*You see someone else when you look
in the mirror—like Snow White's*

*Wicked stepmother—you envy the other
she always has more*

Her voice almost a low *hoo hoo*
a who, more call than response

It's easier

to abandon ship
than it is to walk on water
or, that is, to walk out across the sea
doing what I usually do, which is to sink

it's easier to abandon ship
than to have your legs weighed down
and I ask her why things like birth
and death have to be so painful

and all she says is that they are *real*
then she clarifies
I mean, 'real' in psychoanalytic terms
which, she says, means something else again

I watch myself step into the murk of blue
untroubled by the continents of plastic
I listen for the sound of waves or, that is
for particles turning into waves

and I say, *you are moving forward*
when all I'm doing is sinking with the tide
in this place that's sometimes no-place
that sings me like a siren

The fig tree

When it's cut to the ground
the fig tree

at the edge of her path
re-emerges

next it's poisoned
but another shoot reappears

I remark on it
and she says, in a tone

between frustration
and fury, *it's unkillable*

later, I reconsider her words
about the need to obliterate

my long dead father
who lingers within me

as if my life depends
on his presence

but who, like the fig tree
refuses to die

Someone who isn't

I don't know how to speak or write
something blocks me
like the dog who barks
at someone who isn't there

or the way I'm always searching
for what is missing in me
instead of seeing *you*
as you are

in a dream this morning
my job was to cover
ugly buildings with whitewash
I don't like that I was that person

though in my dream I didn't care
and who am I to judge myself in dreams?
I am writing about you now
even if it's not you I'm writing about

Resistance

Before I go to sleep
I remember that she says
I need to kill the dead

that I have to do this
in order to let
the mourning be

but tonight like other nights
there's resistance and I don't
know what to make of it

still I sense it
in my physiognomy
as clear as this voice

and I recognise
that tonight I'm still
incapable of murder

The first morning

I'm barely awake
I'm still in pyjamas
perhaps I'm still asleep
and have slept through everything

I'm still in a persistent dream
with its insistent howl
and years later I won't know
if I'm one of the bawlers

My sister is yelling
shut up shut up shut up stupid
don't you understand
anything?

But I don't understand
I stare at the window
so much light streams in
it might be biblical

I create and re-create
the fall of light
that surrounds
a shape on the floor

Although much later
—perhaps it's only today
I recognise there never was anything
on the floor by the window

In the collective mania
of the dying father
light streams in the window
as everyone colludes

I'm in my pyjamas
playing my part
my mother howling
blubbering, ululating

And this incremental
inexplicable numbness
—which probably
also comes later

For now my mother flails
a trapped wild bear
who everyone says
I need to protect

In the morning light
my father slips
into the mirror
before it's covered over

I'm already a canary
like the one that used
to fly
around the kitchen

Whose cage was shifted
to the alcove
who would later escape to sky
or the mouth of a cat

Perhaps I've flown
into the mirror
with my father
have become a song of air

While he becomes words
which remain unspoken
then slide
into silence

Words that existed once
but now are only pockets of light
I glide over them
then catch on phrases

Captive in the mirror
as the child who plays at me
becomes proficient
in her role

The howling growling
mammal is anaesthetised
her wound cauterised
and my sister is already Sisyphus

I can see him he's with me, I tell her
she's a tiny exasperated Sisyphus
who'll do anything
to shut the idiot up

To not have to keep
this ball rolling
to not let
the mourning break

Phantoms

According to a friend who teaches economics
everyone who's ever seriously studied the subject
knows that it rests on a false premise
or, that is, that it makes no sense

Still, according to my friend, the world spins
on this fiction, so I find that I too must accept it
even though I barely accept anything
about this place or planet

Not even how the sun
determines to continue each morning
on its predictable trajectory—
doesn't it ever find it all too hard?

And the steadily ever-expanding
nature of the universe—so massive and so aged
how does anyone begin to grapple with this
let alone believe in it?

While closer in, I see that I barely accept
the existence of others or those
who pass me in the street like phantoms
where sometimes we acknowledge each other

At times their words, almost
comprehensible, at others, we might laugh
together, even if it is at different things
the *you* and the *I*, more fiction

Like these hands, that might be me
which maladroitly type then rewrite phrases
they all seem black and white
or, almost real enough

Until I clap and kill those tiny irritating insects
that were always headed for oblivion
and I check myself and my limited
or would you say, fictional compassion

And how is it, that I'm the only one
who's paralysed in these days
where I can't even bring myself
to believe in days?

When the past keeps stretching
further and further out of reach
and everything
has this impenetrable permeability

But just now, the cat is by the door
practising his dark arts again
I find I'm hypnotised
and obediently go to let him in

I may be trapped
by this enchantment
where insistent non-sense
must have its place

The phone rings

and the cat jumps off
my lap and then meows at me

I know that cats don't meow
at other felines, only at humans

I try to think of a way forward
isn't that necessary in a piece of writing?

Not that I mean it that way
the cat, however, is predictably

Indifferent and in the paper today
the obituary for my mother

Which the newspaper neglected
to inform me it was running

Later I do the sudoku on the reverse
and wonder about life's objectives

Car headlights flicker through trees
I'm told will only live a few more years

Things aren't unfolding as they might
the cat remains indifferent

Form

Someone will make a reference
to her age and it's almost funny

since all she sees is the child
who has persevered

when it's clear that others
see her in the form of lines

she sees herself the way
poets are taught to write

or, that is, from
the inside looking out

but instead she's perceived
in realms that shift, like fiction

On arctic foxes and snow owls

If this were a perfect world
then the arctic fox would eat berries
and not hunt baby snow owls

But in this lesser place
where snowy owlets feed
on goslings and songbirds

There are those who say
that animals are much like us
but that they are pure emotion

Except isn't everything analogous
and I don't know, are you an arctic fox
am I a snowy owl?

Magnifications

Before she connected the headphones to the tree
she said, *I've been told that ice cracking*

sounds like a child screaming
I knew she meant this literally

when I listened to the tree I heard a pulse
like the sound of a heart beating, in drips

in that moment things concertinaed
though maybe what I mean is the opposite?

Except someone else was already there
closing it all down

saying, *the only thing you ever hear*
is the magnification of your own sound

Documenting clouds

Even though it's overcast
I spend my day taking photos of clouds
while I know it's been done before

and that this suggests a failure
of imagination on my part
I can't help thinking of each cloud as unique

as I'm re-documenting the heavens
I shift focus, to consider the image of a suited man
carried away by a flock of birds

or that scientist who was speaking
about intelligence, attempting
to define it, outside human terms

he was talking about how birds can find
their way across continents, though people
often can't work out where on earth they are

I'd like to better understand the non-human
but the fact is, I barely grasp our species
with only these thoughts to masquerade as clouds

A photo of a photo

I saw a photograph of a woman holding a reindeer
and the line of the woman's eyes was mimicked

in the caribou's look
so you could see that it was smiling

I was thinking about that smile
as I took a photo of the photo

with my shattered white iphone
then later I had an idea for an artwork

made of broken and abandoned
mobile phones as mine will soon become

how the cracked apple icon
might well read as biblical

but I was also thinking that someone
must have already done this

while later that morning
the creek turned a coffee colour

which they say is the consequence
of erosion and overdevelopment

and everything that's happening here
is happening somewhere else

with all these photographs of photographs
being stored for someone, somewhere

though perhaps I have it all wrong, and was it
the reindeer's laugh that the woman's eyes replicated?

Signs of weakness

today there's a plume of toxic chemicals
and those who are *sensitive*
have been told to stay indoors

they say the fire could burn for days
and the wind is blowing my way
dissipating contaminants into the April air

I read that concerns for the environment
are perceived as feminine
that men may have an unconscious bias

which means they're primed
to see such matters as signs
of weakness, rather than a call to act

and although I try to see myself outside
these prisms, it's like avoiding breathing
chemicals that have spilled into the air

In the air

I know I'm in a bubble of dog walks
and imaginable conversations
that are at times political
at other times inane

the dog drags me
when he's overwhelmed
by trams and buses
but there's no avoiding them

like the plastic
I collect along the road
I don't know how to console
the dog or myself

they say microplastics
are everywhere even in the air
and the herbicide they routinely spray
has also taken root in our bodies

is infused in
what we eat
how to react to this
and not be overwhelmed

how to not strain
at the leash
and run straight into
the path of danger

It was the lightest of touch

or a version of kindness
that arrives and surprises
like a bird emerging

even if that bird has been
observing me for who knows
how long

as if it knows who I am
as if it knows everything about me
even things I'll never understand

except birds do not emerge
for my own
egotistic reasons

even if, just then
one called to me
and even if

this morning
in my mind's eye
I held a hummingbird

while in the afternoon
I saw a map
of the known universe

which looked
more or less
like a feather

but in this morning's version
I was holding a hummingbird
as if it were my heart

Rock

I'm not sure if it's volcanic igneous
or metamorphic
but there's a rock inside my heart

Surely it must be metamorphic
I hear you think, since you probably mix words
like I do, but no matter

The rock is impervious
I go to smash it with a blunt instrument
instead my body weathers the blow

It's not easy to smash a rock
that has no inclination
towards disintegration

And god knows
I've tried other tactics
often watering it away

Except my blubbering
just forms its own cataract
smoothing only the roughest edges

While the rock
itself, refuses
to budge

Instead I've learned to sit
beneath the waterfall
beside an entrance to a cave

Where I do my best to simply be
like that hermit who was stranded
isolated in a desert of his own choosing

Living in a rock
that had as little concern for him
as mine does for me

My rock is firm
and durable
it recognises my mortality

And holds
me in it
while I pretend I am free

In the time

my friend didn't know the one tree
in his backyard was a mulberry
still, there are those who see trees
as *only a green thing that stands in the way*
Blake wrote in seventeen ninety-nine

this week I listened to the sound
of wings fluttering to silence
on a recording of the last ever
pipistrelle bat
which lived
on Christmas Island—

an island
I only remember as a place
where we've imprisoned people—

and I know little
about pipistrelle bats
not even if they liked to sing
in frequencies beyond our reach
as other bats are known to do
It was just the recorded flapping
of the last pipistrelle sounding out
but I thought, *whatever we do*
to other species we're capable
of doing to our own

I was reaching for a mulberry
in the time the pipistrelles vanished
and those on our island prisons half-heard

Dinosaurs

I saw the magic show where children
were a disappearing act

they placed them somewhere
no one could see

fenced in what looked to be
an unvisitable zoo

ordinary children
just like most other children

but who were kept on an island
under lock and key

almost forgotten, not quite disappeared
not yet invisible

the children saw the sea, the stars
and the sky, and they looked

to the birds that came and went
birds, just like most other birds

that were once dinosaurs
and who now fed on smaller birds

I saw the sleight of hand in the magic
when the children wouldn't disappear

but it was incomprehensible
how ordinary hearts turned to stone

Outside

I stand outside
and listen
the currawongs
are making
their usual racket

I think about
how they never
used to be here
and how the lorikeets
are also not local

the police
have raided
the public broadcaster
so nobody can deny
what's happening

the birds
don't belong
here
any more
than my family

but like them
they've settled in
a place
they think
is free

For what seems like weeks

haze covers the city
how to breathe

through the shroud
that mutes everything

an indefinable disconnect
emerges between people

though they all think
similar thoughts

because the pall's too close
too unimaginable

like the *billion* animals
the shroud carries

lingering like a pathetic fallacy
of the earth grieving for itself

In red blankets

The solstice passes but it's still bleak
the days too warm and then too cold

the minister who's responsible says
he wants to put *a positive spin on homelessness*

I'm wondering about the people who camp
on the creek bank, if they're still there

I sometimes see them on Wednesdays
by the tram stop, wrapped in red blankets

almost a vision from *The Handmaid's Tale*
and though I'd like to say I worry about them

the truth is, when I see them, generally
all I worry about is my own safety

the men look at me too closely
with no sense of personal space

as if I have something that they want
I don't return their gaze, instead I protect

what's mine and I'm not sure if this isn't
what happens when it all breaks down

when those who have nothing
are transformed into the thing we fear

It's spring

and all the maddies are emerging
where does all this colour come from anyhow?

I remain a paler variety of myself
while the world outside reimagines

itself beyond chlorophyll into being, buds
and sepals so vivid they're almost startling

meanwhile those problematic Indian mynahs
that you call starlings, keep returning to a nest

under the house's eaves and *you*
ordinarily so easy about life and death

in the *natural* world
as if that place is outside us

you don't have the heart, and instead say
it'd be too cruel to do anything just now

we collude in our flawed version of kindness
allow the dominant birds to nest within our nest

Sway

When it gets too loud in the cafe
I listen to the people around me

A man says
I have this self-loathing
of how trendy I am, I mean as an older man
who's also, you know, a millennial

An elderly woman touches
her husband's wrist and says
I heard a program about trees
about how they communicate
that suggests they're like humans

Then someone else says
You know when everything went quiet
on September 11, scientists near New York
noticed anxiety levels in whales decrease
and that's when they learned
that all our human noise
is distressing to whales

In the background now
the sound of a chainsaw
I think about anxious whales
and also about the couple

The woman's tenderness
when her husband leant on her
as he went to stand up

How as they left I noticed their height
as well as the sway in their walk
the leaves fallen by their feet

3.

Somewhere then

At first there was that collective schadenfreude

the Minister had been diagnosed, there was talk of Johnson and
Bolsonaro

for a moment the idea that this might be a contemporary Passover
miracle

amid other magical thoughts, like those dolphins that had returned to
Venice

except there'd never been dolphins in Venice

but it was early on and a person could believe anything

Blue skies washed Beijing, the Taj Mahal emerged from smog

stillness permeated and the stars shone brighter

There was the potential to see things anew in the pause

since that's how it was seen   as a pause   not a beginning

Besides this wasn't really the beginning, that was much earlier

the incomprehensible footage of Wuhan

where people were dragged from their homes

which made no sense, or made sense only as unnecessary cruelty

perhaps that was the start—even if the start was well before then another place, another time or like somewhere

I usually place myself, which is left of centre

This, though, was more like the assassination of Archduke Ferdinand

or not like that, but something unrelated, invisible, molecular

like the miniscule bears that live in the water we drink

or the microplastics we take in, without knowing we're breathing them

a microbe that effected a tipping point

a bat whose habitat had disappeared

and in the park there was conjecture, about what language

a planet might use to communicate its wrath

The bushfires had only just been extinguished

there'd been tornadoes in Tennessee

perhaps the billion animals were exacting their revenge?

At that start then, it was as if there might be something to learn

that it might be for some greater good

the bank was printing money

and there was even talk of a universal basic income

it was fleeting, that moment, that start—

Days have rewritten days now

masks are falling to the ground

a speaker says, *Beginnings are hard to locate*

endings are more definitive

then they add, *Now is not a good time to die*

People address empty chairs

they might otherwise be storing for Elijah.

My relationship to profanity may be different to yours

Provided I said it in English
I could say whatever I liked

I would say *fuck you* and neither
my mother nor grandmother would care

I knew words had power
even if they were emptied of meaning

So whenever I'd hear the English word
cholera, it sounded soft, almost deferential

While I'd become accustomed
to its Slavic cousin, a guttural *cho-lera*

Where the *cho* is ho, tough and aspirated
or spat out in tones of everyday fury

An available curse that I used
because I wasn't supposed to

Like *psia krew* which meant *dog's blood*
and was even less comprehensible

Since I loved dogs, yet saying it
was more like saying *damn*

A word I never connected with damnation
though *cho-lera* went beyond blood and disease

To mean something more like *this living hell*
or *ten jasna cholera*—that *SOB!* or the *bastard!*

More words I didn't understand
yet accepted as illogical

And though I was experienced in pointless rage
I didn't know about the curse of plagues

I'd never worn a mask
and until last year I didn't think I would

These days mine's a warm accessory
hand-embroidered in India

It often elicits compliments
while it covers half my face

And now when I say *cholera*
I understand the derivation

Someone threw a rock

through a family home
then painted *Covid 19—China Die* on the garage

While last night I dreamt that I left my bicycle
at a grocery shop and instead I had to fly home

This morning, with work
no longer a primary paradigm

I notice something form between
the half-asleep, half-paralysed

That could be a crack
though later it might just be patched over

Still, now nothing seems as solid as before
so why did I dream of flying last night?

The house turns to sticks
—the garden a mirage

As the half-awake
half-asleep thing takes hold

And there are those who seek scapegoats
because rocks have always been an answer

So tell me, how was it, that in my dream
I was flying?

And did I tell you

I don't want to have to live in a world
where people fight in the supermarket
over toilet paper

I don't want to have to live in a world
where people fight anywhere
over toilet paper

Meanwhile a voice on the radio says
—*We are witnessing*
the beginning of the end

But this is not news
and besides I don't want
to have to live in a world

Where I have to distance myself
from everyone
or even from these thoughts

While the whole world ails
and the only talk
is of the ailment of humans

Still, I remember holding my mother
as she lay there
already gone

This was before they came to take her
with their tired suits
and their well-worn phrases

And what does it matter
that she'd been a doctor
or if that's why I think of her now

In conjunction with
pestilence and plague
or this anger

All of which might be
the appropriate language
of a precarious world's passing

Like swallows

the headline reads
—a small native bird

(a small *unnamed* native bird)
has been observed dying en masse

then in the afternoon
I see footage of a cloud forest

that is still in peril and my first thought is
—some places are constantly threatened

a war that is never won—but fought
then fought again and again and again

a poem reread
or overlooked in time

or as seen through mist
that might be a cloud forest

not a mass of small birds
—dead native tree martins

that look like swallows
all of this in its own time—our time

not outside of it, not perpetual
like the sense of being lost in the mist

but more like the resignation
that comes with age

one moment swallows another
those small birds have a name

The language of birds

I would have to speak the language of birds
to let him know that some flying things

see faster than we do
that we can never experience the world as they do

I would have to let him know
that although I'm born of this place

I have no knowledge of
its language

even if where I walk there's a creek
(more often it's a slew of plastic)

and though I'm beginning to recognise
different songs

among the grasses I can only discern
the jagged-edged lomandra

still I try my best *to do no harm*
to simply let the earth sink underfoot

to steady the despair
which sometimes rises

I would have to tell him
about the eight-year-old who lives next door

who is part-*Inuit* and how much I like saying that word
is it because it reminds me of the word *intuit?*

I would have to let him know
about the girl's mother who is pregnant

and how she said, *I feel like a whale*
just when I was thinking that people

use language in ways
that reveal their own stories

even if there are those, like him
who are more difficult to read

though not as impossible
as birds

Curfew

Although she didn't recognise the constellations
the night sky was under her skin

Once she'd paid a man two dollars
to look through a telescope

He said, *the sky's so clear you'll see Saturn*
she'd made out a speck with a ring

A speck that had stayed within her
but now there was less light spilling

Into the night sky and she didn't know
whether this improved darkness would pass

In her mind she played then replayed
scenes of armoured police swarming

On protesters forcing them into white vans
she wasn't sure why she thought of the ants

In the hallway, she'd tackled them with a concerted
violence that she preferred not to acknowledge

The vision, like the ants, kept returning and returning
even now, she didn't comprehend it any better

Than she understood her own self, under her skin
an inky blue-black—with bursts of insight

People wore masks over their usual masks
they looked away more than before, as if terrorised

It was a time of dark skies
even as the constellations cleared

Dandelions

It's horses for courses, she says
as if we're talking about food
and not identity

that afternoon when I use the word
obsequious you tell me
it's not the word I mean

though later I check and I see
that it is, and later again
when we're talking about *Boxing Day*

I search its origins—how the rich
used to box unwanted goods for their servants
I say, *I heard Santa Claus is an invention*

of Coca-cola Amatil
and Jo says, *Yes, even the colours are the same*
then adds, *Everything's about marketing*

I'm still thinking about courses
and horses the following morning
as the world reimagines itself

I'm unsure why everything
doesn't simply scatter
like dandelions to the wind

or to put it another way
I might write about the sky
as if it were something to grasp

but I'm further down a track
than I thought I would be
and my main wealth is in words

or phrases, strewn like weeds

Those people in metros in places with names you can't properly pronounce

They tether their cats and babies to their bodies
hold their plastic bags in tight fists

Their faces sometimes poised
often resigned, possibly haunted

Though perhaps the haunting
is your own invention

Because you see them as if
from another time—that other place

Like the child with her arms
in the air surrendering

Why would anyone do that
to a child of three you ask yourself?

As if you were in that other place
that other time—not this now

You think about those people, the women
with their names like Maria, Olga

And Ania—your lost original name
how you might be one of them

But it's all too close to Maria, the enigma
that you recognise as your mother

Who emerged from somewhere there
in much the same way

A child in the snow
with her arms in the air

The ways of crows

Above you a murder of crows
(if it is a murder and not a murmuration?)
birds circling shrieking Hitchcock-like

Among them you see a magpie
which only adds to the confusion
the background shifts forward

Is destabilising like a flood or gunfire
a woman is saying
*they aren't even **good** birds*

And you recognise how she classifies them
into good versus bad
—not that you understand this *good*

Crows are intelligent
(if that matters?)
they are said to be Bunjil's messengers

Perhaps like us, they see god
in their own image
still their formation is ominous bleak

Later you go over the ways of crows
how they remember human faces
years after seeing them

And recognise people
even when their faces
are completely covered over

Bear grudges just like we do
pass them on to their offspring
which we also do

They understand analogies
circle is to square
apple is to pear

Crows prey on other birds
are oleaginous
and you suspect

They may also have their own
reasons for murder
so perhaps this is an army

This cacophony
of unmusical screeches
uncontained wild

But it is not an army unless—
unless it's an army of schoolboys
unless—*but you know nothing of war*

Meanwhile, like you, everyone keeps walking
as though not much were occurring
just another ordinary enigma

And the context you're trying to evoke now
as if to tame the murder
into your own schema

There are cities that are rubble
the animals in the zoo traumatised
by the sound of artillery

A man risks his life to save the kangaroos
but other creatures remain
the bison, the pelican, the toucans, the people

The way I need to write now

I won't look in the mirror and remain unseen
or be the owl who witnesses like Echo unheard
whose features aren't read
in the watery reflection
that the narcissist treats as solid

The way I need to write is to reflect
the violence of this moment—to strike so hard
that nothing's left of the person or the reflection
just debris or the stain of bloodied water
while everyone dies of thirst and all hope is obliterated

Then I'll need to trap the owl who may be Echo
but forget mythology and history—let it re-create itself
I don't want a witness after all
I'll have to disembowel and eat the owl from eye socket to claw
I need to do this in my writing even if I'm a vegetarian

It's only when I engulf the avian cavity
I'll sense the remnant of forest and stars
that once watched from within the creature not as mirror
or metaphor but the untamed as it exists in each
then I'll efface even this to nothing more than matter

Because this is the way things are right now
and where ordinarily I turn away from darkness
as if somehow not looking or refusing to see
the same way that avoiding the truth is still lying
but somehow, just now

I'm dumb to the sounds the world is witnessing
the mass graves, the rapes, the Bucha, the everything
as if to stop all of what's happening from happening
as if to stop an owl from seeing
as if to stop—

Seven facts

1. A picture of boys
   in trucks holding weapons
   that look like toys

2. An exposé of neo-Nazis
   whose plan is
   to mate with Jewish bitches

3. A videotape
   of a family's illegal
   engagement party

4. My first thought
   why give those boys
   a reason?

5. Someone else's
   immediate response
   gas them all

6. The knowledge
   those boys or men
   don't need a reason

7. The realisation
   I live my life
   as if they do

Goodnight moon

I keep mistaking sunflowers for humans
not that I mistake humans for sunflowers

then I see photos of polar bears
at an abandoned house in the Arctic circle

which was once a weather station
the bears are doing what polar bears do

even as they play in their doll's house
mother bear makes pancakes

while father bear smokes on the porch
the cubs gaze out through the windows

with their polar bear look of wonderment
come bedtime they'll read their *Goodnight moon*

then drift from icefloes to sunflowers
and other lives that came then went

In the twilight

the girl points to a question mark
the clouds have formed
behind my head

I photograph the question
as if to capture
the moment

like the boy
in the embroidery
whose arms

are perpetually lifted
to catch a bird in flight
that is forever out of reach

a praying mantis is on the door frame
living a life as necessary
as mine

Sunflowers

upside down
on the sunflowers
the rainbow lorikeets
gorge on seeds,
beneath them
the plants
sway
and
the
weight
of
the
world's
darkness
ebbs

Acknowledgements

A treatment, Peter Porter Prize 2022 Longlist

Sophia does not hold up the world, ACU Poetry Prize 2021 Shortlist, published in *ACU Prize for Poetry Anthology* 2021

On seeing a woman who resembles me in a photo of the liberation of Ravensbrück, 2nd Prize Darebin Literary Awards

Playing scrabble with my mother published in *Not Very Quiet* 2020 (online)

From a remove published in *Cordite Poetry Review* 35: Custom 2009

Synonyms, Liquid Amber Poetry Prize 2022 Longlist, published in *Poetry of Encounter: The Liquid Amber Prize Anthology* 2022

The first morning published in *Grieve: Stories and Poems of Grief and Loss* volume 10, 2022

On arctic foxes and snow owls published in *Burrow* 2021 (online)

Magnifications published in *Red Room Poetry*, Writing Water 2020 (online)

Documenting clouds and *In the time* published in *Science Write Now* edition 6, 2022 (online)

Sway, ACU Poetry Prize 2019 Shortlist, published in *Solace ACU Poetry Awards* 2019

And did I tell you and *Curfew* published in *Lockdown Poetry: The Covid Long Haul*, Liquid Amber Press 2021

Those people in metros with names you can't properly pronounce published in *Wordpeace* digital issue: 7.2 summer/fall 2022

I'm over the moon to be published by Upswell. Terri-ann White represents a dream in waking life, her support has sustained me.

I'm grateful to Kelly Somers for editing this collection and for her attention to detail in that role.

My thanks to Gayelene Carbis, Anne Carson, Emilie Collyer, Jen Compton, Anne Elvey, Michelle Leber, Rose Lucas and Belinda Rule for letting me attend what was originally their Bayside poetry workshop group, despite the fact that I live nowhere near the bay.

Sue Saliba has consistently supported my writing and my visual art, I'm so grateful to her for this, as well as for our friendship and for how she views the natural world.

Hilma Wolitzer read poems in this collection, I'm very appreciative of that support as well as her incredible writing.

Many thanks to Damen O'Brien for his poem *Atlas Carried the World*, which inspired the poem *Sophia does not hold up the world*.

Alex Skovron, Lorender Freeman, Janine Perlman, Julie Gittus, Elizabeth Newman, Jenny McGregor, Anita Beckman, Kim Kingston, Angela Lane and Rachel Edwardson read various poems and were supportive of my pursuit of this impossible profession.

My thanks to Esther Faye as someone who is supposed to know.

Both Odette and Lucienne Shenfield supported me by reading various drafts of the poems and the manuscript when it would have been enough to simply be who they are. And, likewise, though also different, for Andrew McGregor.

About Upswell

Upswell Publishing was established in 2021 by Terri-ann White as a not-for-profit press. A perceived gap in the market for distinctive literary works in fiction, poetry and narrative non-fiction was the motivation. In her years as a bookseller, writer and then publisher, Terri-ann has maintained a watch on literary books and the way they insinuate themselves into a cultural space and are then located within our literary and cultural inheritance. She is interested in making books to last: books with the potential to still be noticed, and noted, after decades and thus be ripe to influence new literary histories.

About this typeface

Book designer Becky Chilcott chose
Foundry Origin not only as a strong,
carefully considered, and dependable
typeface, but also to honour her late
friend and mentor, type designer Freda
Sack, who oversaw the project. Designed
by Freda's long-standing colleague,
Stuart de Rozario, much like Upswell
Publishing, Foundry Origin was created
out of the desire to say something new.

www.ingramcontent.com/pod-product-compliance
Lightning Source LLC
Chambersburg PA
CBHW030847090426
42737CB00009B/1130